Soldiers of the Khyber Rifles, an armed constabulary on the North West Frontier. In this photograph by Frank Bremner of c.1895 they are armed with Snider breech-loaders – a very late use of this old weapon, but typical of the policy of arming Indian paramilitary forces with weapons that were obsolete.

British Military Rifles

1800-2000

Peter Duckers

A Shire book

Published in 2005 by Shire Publications Ltd,
Cromwell House, Church Street, Princes Risborough,
Buckinghamshire HP27 9AA, UK.
(Website: www.shirebooks.co.uk)

Copyright © 2005 by Peter Duckers.
First published 2005.
Shire Album 445. ISBN 0 7478 0633 0.
Peter Duckers is hereby identified as the author of this
work in accordance with Section 77 of the Copyright,
Designs and Patents Act 1988.

British Library Cataloguing in Publication Data:
Duckers, Peter
British military rifles 1800–2000. – (Shire album; 445)
1. Great Britain. Army – Equipment –
History – 19th century
2. Great Britain. Army – Equipment –
History – 20th century
3. Rifles – Great Britain – History
I. Title 623.4'425'0941
ISBN-10: 0 7478 0633 0

Cover: *A British soldier advancing into action with rifle and fixed bayonet. (From a patriotic postcard of 1914.)*

ACKNOWLEDGEMENTS
The author would like to thank the Trustees of the Shropshire Regimental Museum for
permission to use the rifles and images held in the collection in Shrewsbury Castle. The
photographs on pages 29 (bottom) and 31 (top left) are reproduced by kind permission
of the Imperial War Museum. The photograph on page 8 is acknowledged to S. Martin.
Many individual collectors have helped with weapons, information and images and he
would particularly like to extend his thanks to Mr Paul Ridgley and Mr Mick Crumplin
for their help in this respect.

Printed in Great Britain by CIT Printing Services, Press Buildings,
Merlins Bridge, Haverfordwest, Pembrokeshire SA61 1XF.

Contents

A British sniper in action in Normandy in 1944. Throughout the twentieth century trained snipers used a range of more accurate rifles than those issued to other soldiers. Their development and use is a separate study in itself.

The earliest 'guns'

Invented in China before AD 1100, gunpowder was introduced into western Europe or developed independently there by the mid thirteenth century. Its potential as an explosive was not lost on early producers and gunpowder was soon in evidence on the battlefield. Its use to fire projectiles is recorded as early as the 1320s, and artillery pieces and 'hand-cannons' were in action in Italy by the 1330s and at the Battle of Crécy in 1346. The oldest *surviving* hand-guns are made of cast bronze and date to the late fourteenth century.

The earliest hand-held firearm was simply a tube of iron or bronze, sealed at one end and open at the other, sometimes mounted on a wooden handle or *stock*. Gunpowder and some form of projectile, such as shaped metal or stone shot, were loaded into the open end. The powder was ignited by a flame through a small *touch-hole* at the sealed end and the consequent explosion of the gunpowder blew out the contents – hopefully in the direction of the enemy. Not surprisingly, given the variable quality of gunpowder mixtures and variations in the manufacture of the weapons, proper aiming was difficult, ranges varied enormously and misfires must have been common. The phrase 'hoist with one's own petard' – blown up by your own bomb – recalls the dangers of using early weapons charged with gunpowder.

A medieval hand-gunner, from a mid-fifteenth-century manuscript. He fires the tube by applying a hot iron rod to the touch-hole. Note the handle or stock and the fact that he can only 'aim' the gun with one hand – not an ideal way to support a powerful weapon or to ensure any accuracy of direction!

A hand-gunner of c.1500. This weapon at least has a solid wooden stock, though how it was actually fired is not clear from this Victorian rendition of a medieval drawing.

The first type of 'long-arm' that looks anything like a modern firearm did not develop until the fifteenth century. From *c.*1400, and increasingly during the sixteenth century, the *matchlock* was in use. A slow-burning length of cord held in a *linstock* was pulled on to the touch-hole by a simple 'serpentine' trigger mechanism, enabling the user to grip and point the weapon with both hands.

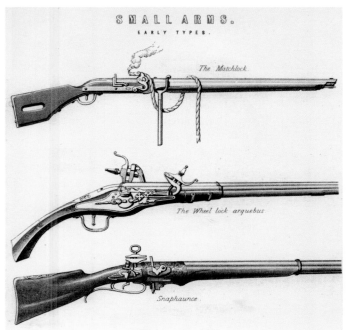

SMALL ARMS.

EARLY TYPES.

The Matchlock

The Wheel lock arquebus

Snaphaunce.

Early firearms showing different types of firing mechanism – the matchlock, the wheel-lock (which used a clockwork mechanism) and the snaphaunce, an early type of flintlock. All were eventually superseded by a more developed flintlock system.

A musketeer of c.1607 – very much the look of a similar soldier of the English Civil War. He carries an arquebus – a type of matchlock musket. Note the burning slow-match (top right), the rest for the barrel in his right hand, and the measured charges of powder and shot-flask hanging from his bandolier. (From 'The Exercise of Arms' by Jacob de Gheyn, 1607)

Although types of matchlock remained the basic long-arm well into the seventeenth century (being used, for example, in the English Civil War), the *flintlock* had come into use by the late sixteenth century. Despite being slow to develop after 1600, from the middle of the seventeenth century several varieties were in use throughout western Europe, where the flintlock mechanism was to predominate for nearly two hundred years. Not until the 1840s was it superseded by the *percussion* system.

The table below shows the different phases through which long-arms used by the British Army have passed since the end of the seventeenth century.

Long-arms since c.1690

c.1690–1800	Muzzle-loading, single-shot, smooth-bore flint-lock musket
1800–1840	Muzzle-loading, single-shot, smooth-bore flint-lock musket and early rifles
c.1840–1867	Muzzle-loading, single-shot, percussion musket and percussion rifle
1867–c.1895	Breech-loading single-shot rifle
1888–1957	Bolt-action magazine rifle
1957–	Self-loading or automatic magazine rifle

A typical flintlock mechanism – here on a Brown Bess of 1762. When it was fired, a piece of flint, held in the jaws of the 'cock', struck a metal plate (the 'anvil' or 'frizzen'), pushing it backwards and directing a shower of sparks into the 'pan', which contained a small charge of gunpowder. The ignition of this charge set off, via the 'touch-hole', the main powder charge in the barrel, which fired the ball.

Flintlock muskets, *c.*1690–1840

The first flintlock muskets used by the British Army as standard issue date to the 1690s, during the rebuilding of the army under William III. They were modelled on types used by the French, who are credited with developing the flintlock as a military long-arm. For almost 140 years from *c.*1704 British infantry relied upon a flintlock properly called the 'Tower' musket, but whose various types were universally known as the 'Brown Bess'.

There were many variants of Brown Bess, but in general those used by the British Army fall into four distinct patterns:

1. *c.*1710–68: the 'long' land musket, with a barrel measuring 46 inches in length
2. *c.*1720–94: the 'short' land musket, with a barrel measuring 42 inches in length
3. *c.*1794–*c.*1815: the 'India Pattern' musket
4. 1802–40: the 'New Land Pattern' or 'New Land Service' musket

Left: *The New Land Pattern musket, introduced during the Napoleonic Wars.*

Right: *Drilling with the Brown Bess musket, from an eighteenth-century manual.*

A replica of an early cartridge. Composed of stiff paper (hence 'cartridge paper') and holding a measured charge of powder and a lead ball, cartridges could be made by soldiers in their spare time. The soldier bit the end off and poured first the powder and then the ball into the barrel, using the ramrod to push down the paper tube as wadding to stop the contents falling out of the barrel. When the musket was fired, the wadding burned and fouled the barrel. Not until the invention of breech-loaders did cartridges significantly alter in look, with the eventual introduction of metal cartridge cases for the Snider rifle.

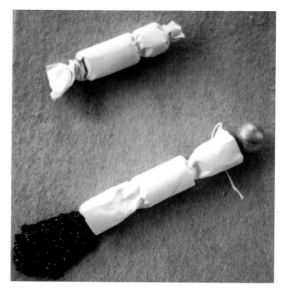

In the first half of the eighteenth century both the 'long' and 'short' land muskets were in use, but from 1768 the 'short' pattern was universally adopted by British infantry and the 'long' pattern was phased out. At the outset of the French Wars in 1793 a shortage of weapons led to the adoption of the East India Company version, with its shorter, 39 inch barrel. The New Land Pattern musket was a better-made version of the India Pattern and remained in use until the Brown Bess was superseded c.1840.

These muskets had a large calibre of about three-quarters of an inch, firing a heavy lead ball, but were not especially accurate or reliable – damp or damage to the flint could prevent proper firing. When clean, and with a tight-fitting ball, the musket was accurate to a range of approximately 80–100 yards but as the black powder available at the time caused the barrel to foul easily it was necessary to use loose-fitting musket balls and these were not capable of being fired with any accuracy beyond about 30 yards. For this reason European armies (which all used similar muskets) were trained in mass firing and volley firing rather than in individual marksmanship.

The first British rifles, 1775–1840

Rifles are firearms whose barrels are *rifled* – they have a series of parallel or spiral grooves running down their inside length; a bullet guided by these grooves will travel in a straighter line and, if the rifling is spiralled, will spin, aiding its accuracy in flight. Rifled firearms were more accurate over a longer range and, with a spinning bullet, packed more of a punch.

The principle of rifling was recognised as early as *c.*1520 in the German states but because rifles were much more difficult to make than muskets it was not until the early seventeenth century that they entered military use, and not until the eighteenth century were they used in any quantity. Rifles were first developed as effective weapons in Austria and the German states by woodland huntsmen and later equipped the first *light infantry* troops – skirmishers and sharpshooters – in the armies of those countries. Regiments of German and Austrian riflemen, known as *jaegers* after their origins as hunters, were employed in the European wars of the eighteenth century. German settlers took the idea of the rifled musket to America, where they became favoured weapons in the woodlands of New England and elsewhere. The famous *Kentucky rifle* is one example.

The British Army adopted rifles only slowly in the eighteenth century. Once a complex system of production, training and use had been established around one type of weapon – such as the Brown Bess – it proved difficult to introduce a new concept in weapons and drills. The rifle remained for fifty years only on the periphery of British Army use.

In the early eighteenth century the British experimented with light infantry units – lightly armed, fast-moving soldiers,

Riflemen of the 52nd Light Infantry and the 95th Rifles in action during the Peninsular War (from a contemporary print after Charles Hamilton Smith).

trained as marksmen and skirmishers, for whom the rifle would have been the ideal weapon. Even so, only small numbers of rifles (made in continental Europe) were issued. The Royal American Regiment, raised in 1756 and later to become the 60th King's Royal Rifle Corps, had only sixteen rifles in service by 1758. As long as speed of movement, not accuracy of firepower, remained the ideal, these specialist troops tended to be equipped simply with lighter muskets (such as *fusils*) rather than with rifles; and it was not until the effectiveness of the rifle was demonstrated in North America in the Seven Years War of 1756–63 that it slowly began to gain acceptance.

The Ferguson rifle, 1776–80

The British Army's experiences in North America slowly opened the door to greater use of the rifle. The first British flintlock rifle to be tested in war – and a breech-loader at that – was designed by Captain Patrick Ferguson (1744–80). Ferguson, a career officer, was a renowned marksman and after being invalided home from the West Indies in 1774 he devoted his time to the development of a novel type of weapon. His new rifle was demonstrated in April 1776 before an influential group of officers and politicians, who were impressed with its performance, speed of loading (Ferguson claimed seven shots a minute) and accuracy. As a result, the Master General of the Ordnance ordered that Ferguson's rifle, to be manufactured in Birmingham, should be tested 'in the field' by the British Army, then beginning its campaign against the rebellious American colonies.

The Ferguson rifle was revolutionary not only as a rifle but also as a breech-loader. Too few were made to give their capabilities a fair test in the American Revolutionary War and examples are now very rare indeed.

In March 1777 Ferguson was given just one hundred men for training with his new rifle. They crossed to North America and first saw action at Brandywine Hill in Pennsylvania on 11th September. Unfortunately, after serving in several engagements, Ferguson was seriously wounded and the casualties among his riflemen were severe, which led to the unit's disbandment. Ferguson returned to the war in America but was killed in October 1780 and the Army's enthusiasm for his rifle seems to have died with him.

With its rate of fire and accuracy, Ferguson's rifle was well suited to the sort of warfare the British faced in North America but it was never produced in sufficient numbers to prove its

The Ferguson's flintlock mechanism, showing the breech open for loading. The breech was opened by using the trigger-guard as a winding-handle to lower a plug, exposing the breech chamber. Once a ball and powder charge had been loaded, the plug was wound back into place to close the breech.

value on campaign and too few specialists were trained in its use. The Ferguson was quickly dropped from the armament of the British Army and examples of the rifle – some of which were made for the East India Company and some for sporting use – are now exceptionally rare.

The Baker rifle, 1800–40

Overall length	45.8 inches (1163 mm)
Barrel length	30 inches (759 mm)
Weight	approximately 9.5 pounds (4.08 kg)
Range	up to 450 yards; accurate 200–300 yards
Calibre	.625 (the same as in many carbines of the day)
Magazine	none: single-shot muzzle-loader
Rate of fire	approximately two rounds per minute

The first rifle to be extensively used by the British Army was the famous Baker rifle. Designed by Ezekiel Baker, a London weapons maker and later arms contractor to the Board of Ordnance, it saw service between 1800 and *c*.1840.

Tested at Woolwich in 1799–1800, the rifle was adopted by the British Army in February 1800. During the Napoleonic Wars Britain's new Experimental Corps of Riflemen (later to become the famous Rifle Brigade), as well as rifle companies in some Line and Volunteer regiments, were armed with this highly regarded weapon. It was used to great effect during the Peninsular War of 1808–14 and at Waterloo in 1815. Its accuracy over the fairly long range (for its day) of 200–300 yards is well attested in a number of accounts by riflemen but its quality varied depending on where the component parts were produced; mass production clearly led to falling standards in

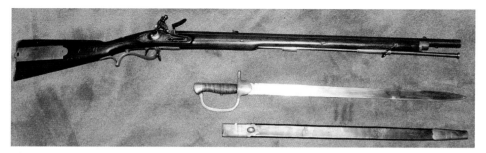

The Baker rifle, with the distinctive 'sword-bayonet' originally issued with it. This gave a longer 'reach' to the rifle in close combat and was equally capable of being used as a weapon in its own right. Later on, standard 'socket bayonets' were used.

some cases. It could also be a slow weapon to load: for the bullet to achieve an airtight fit into the rifling, it had to be set into a greased 'patch' of cloth or leather and hammered down the barrel using the ramrod and a small mallet, which riflemen used to carry. This cumbersome system was soon abandoned and the bullet pushed home simply with the ramrod. Indeed, riflemen also carried smooth-bore musket balls for fast loading in action, but these tended to foul the barrel and were not very accurate.

In general, the Baker was slower to use than the conventional musket – about two rounds per minute in the hands of an experienced rifleman – which was another reason for official reluctance to adopt the rifle as a universal arm. Nevertheless, it remained in service well into the 1830s (when superseded by the Brunswick) and many were produced for use by the East

A print by Harry Payne showing an incident in which Thomas Plunkett of the 95th Rifles steadied his rifle and shot dead the French general Colbert at long range – one of many stories from the Peninsular War that attested the accuracy of the Baker rifle.

The lock, trigger and trigger-guard (with its distinctive hand-grip) of a Baker rifle, shown in the 'fired' position, with the pan open.

India Company. Smaller versions were also adopted by some cavalry regiments.

A breech-loading version of the Baker, first produced in 1817 and known as the Sartoris rifle (after its inventor, Urbanus Sartoris), was not extensively adopted, though some were issued to Volunteer units.

Note: in the following sections initial statistics should be taken to refer to the standard 'issue' weapon of the type. There are in each category many variations in size, weight, calibre and so on, as some were short-lived experimental versions and others produced for different forces, such as police, colonial police, colonial forces, Volunteers or the Royal Navy.

ADVANCED GUARD

AND

OUTPOST DUTIES

FOR RIFLEMEN.

BY
COLONEL L. V. SWAINE,
AND
CAPTAIN WILLOUGHBY VERNER,
RIFLE BRIGADE.

LONDON:
W. H. ALLEN AND CO., 13 WATERLOO PLACE,
PALL MALL. S.W.
———
1889.

(All Rights Reserved.)

A booklet on 'Advanced Guard and Outpost Duties for Riflemen'. The gradual introduction of the rifle necessitated the introduction of new practices and drills. However, by the time of this booklet (intended for the Rifle Volunteers in 1889) all infantrymen were in effect 'riflemen'.

Percussion rifles

The Brunswick rifle, 1837–51

Overall length	46 inches (1168 mm)
Barrel length	29.4 inches (747 mm)
Weight	9 pounds 6 ounces (4.20 kg)
Range	accurate to approximately 300 yards
Calibre	.704
Magazine	none: single-shot muzzle-loader
Rate of fire	approximately two rounds per minute

In the 1830s and 1840s the British Army continued to use smooth-bore muskets, eventually with the new percussion system that was then coming into use. Examples are the 1838, 1839 and 1842 patterns, designed by the gunsmith George Lovell. The 1842-pattern percussion musket was the last smooth-bore to be issued to line regiments and many remained in use for the next twenty years. But the search for an accurate

The percussion lock: cocked, ready to fire. The percussion system, developed by the French and improved by the Reverend Alexander Forsyth in Britain, came into use in the British Army in the 1840s. The system involved the hammer striking a percussion cap – shaped like a small top-hat – which was filled with an explosive compound such as fulminate of mercury. This exploded the cap, which was attached to the breech by a hollow nipple, and that explosion detonated the powder charge in the barrel and fired the ball. It was a great improvement on the flintlock mechanism. It did not rely on flints (whose quality and performance could vary enormously) and was a sealed system less prone to problems with damp and reliable in wet weather. The percussion caps were light to carry and easy to use.

The Brunswick rifle. This heavy percussion rifle, which took its name from the German state of Brunswick, replaced the Baker. The idea of arming all regiments of the British Army with the rifle had not then been put into practice, and the Brunswick was issued to rifle regiments only, such as The Rifle Brigade. Later versions were, however, issued to a few other units and to the Royal Navy.

The percussion lock in closed or fired position. Note the official 'Crown/VR' and '1858/Tower' marks.

and modern rifle as a universal replacement for the old smooth-bore musket continued.

The British Army's first percussion rifle, known as the Brunswick rifle, followed designs by Captain Berners of the army of the German state of Brunswick. Improved by George Lovell in 1831, the Brunswick went into production in January 1837 as 'Lovell's Improved Brunswick Rifle' and was initially issued only to The Rifle Brigade. Its barrel had two rifling grooves and it fired a distinctive 'belted ball' – a bullet with a raised rib around it, which fitted into and gripped the deep rifling. Variant types with 33 inch barrels were produced after 1840 – a lighter version for use by sergeants in Guards' regiments and a much heavier model of .796 calibre for use by the Royal Navy.

The Brunswick did not remain in service with British forces for very long; although some continued to be used in India into the 1860s they were generally superseded in the 1850s by the Minié and Enfield rifles.

The butts and trigger mechanisms of the Brunswick rifle and the 1860 Enfield.

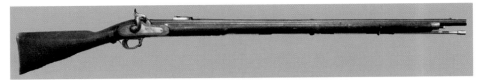

The Minié rifle, adopted by many European countries and the United States after 1849. It was the first rifle intended to be issued to all British regiments, not just to specific Rifle units. However, it had been superseded by the Enfield before all units of the army had been equipped with it.

The Minié rifle, 1851–60

Overall length	54.9 inches (1394 mm)
Barrel length	38.4 inches (975 mm)
Weight	9 pounds 1 ounce (4.11 kg)
Range	up to 1000 yards
Calibre	.702
Magazine	none: single-shot muzzle-loader
Rate of fire	approximately two rounds per minute

Designed by a French officer, Claude-Etienne Minié, this rifle was introduced into the French army after 1849 and quickly taken up by several European nations and the United States. Supported by George Lovell's recommendation, the Minié was approved for service with the British Army in October 1851 – in one of the last acts of the Duke of Wellington as Commander in Chief – and was the first rifle intended to be issued to *all* British regiments, and not just Rifle units. It was known in the British service as the 'Rifle Musket, Pattern 1851'.

It became renowned for its accuracy, which was the result of Minié's rifling system and the new design of a shaped bullet – the first to move away from the ages-old spherical 'ball' form. The rifling grooves deepened from muzzle to breech and the heavy conical bullet had three grooves, filled with tallow, and a conical cavity at its base. Because the bullet was slightly narrower than the rifle bore, it could easily be dropped into the barrel – a great advance in speed of loading – and, when it was

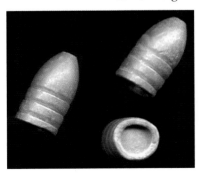

fired, the gunpowder gases caused the bullet to expand and grip the rifling grooves so that it travelled with greater accuracy.

The Minié was extensively, but not exclusively, used in the Crimean War of 1854–6 but, despite the fact that it was highly regarded by its users, it did not have a long service life with the British Army, being superseded by the 1853 Pattern Enfield rifle.

Minié bullets, with their distinctive grooves.

The Minié rifle in use during the Crimean War. (Photograph by Roger Fenton; private collection.)

The Enfield rifle, 1853–67

Overall length	55.3 inches (1405 mm)
Barrel length	38.4 inches (975 mm); shorter version: 33 inches (840 mm)
Weight	8 pounds 14 ounces (3.85 kg); shorter version: 8 pounds 4 ounces (3.15 kg)
Range	800–1000 yards; very accurate to 500 yards
Calibre	.577
Magazine	none: single-shot muzzle-loader
Rate of fire	approximately two rounds per minute

This percussion rifle was produced by the Royal Small Arms Factory at Enfield in Middlesex in 1853. The last muzzle-loading rifle to be extensively used by the British Army, it was designed to supersede the Minié and saw active service in the Crimean War (alongside the Minié), in the Indian Mutiny of 1857–8 and in China in 1856–60. It was designated the 1853 Pattern Enfield 'rifle-musket', because the first version (the 'three-band' Enfield, after the three retaining bands round the

The 1853 'three-band' Enfield rifle, said to be far in advance of any yet issued to the British Army. Its use began in the latter stages of the Crimean War and it was also used in the Indian Mutiny and in China.

Above: *Soldiers in the Crimea, c.1856, armed with Enfield rifles. (From a photograph by Roger Fenton; private collection.)*

Left: *An example of the bullet fired by the Enfield rifle. It was the 'greased cartridges' used with this rifle that contributed to the outbreak of the Indian Mutiny in 1857. The cartridges had to be bitten open to pour the powder down the barrel. Rumours (never fully denied) that they were greased with pork or beef fat outraged the religious sensitivities of both Hindu and Muslim soldiers and helped spark the mutiny of the Bengal army – with terrible consequences.*

barrel) retained the longer length and weight typical of a musket, but with a rifled barrel.

Following its use in the Crimea a number of modifications were imposed, with several new types being produced – the 1856, 1858 and 1860 Patterns. The last two were smaller than the 1853 original, with an overall length of approximately 48.7 inches (1237 mm) and with alterations to the rifling, sights, ramrod and hammer. These shorter patterns are often called 'two-band' Enfields and most of these 'short' rifles were issued to Rifle regiments and to sergeants of infantry units. *Carbine* versions (shortened rifles for use by cavalry, mounted troops, the Royal Artillery and colonial forces) were produced from 1856-7 onwards.

The later Enfield percussion rifle, in this case the shorter, 'two-band' Enfield of the 1860 Pattern.

The **Lancaster rifle**, introduced in 1855 and issued only to the Sappers and Miners, was similar to the 1853 Enfield but with a 32 inch barrel with an unusual straight *oval* bore of .577.

Breech-loading rifles

The Snider rifle, 1867–74

Overall length	54.1 inches (1374 mm)
Barrel length	36.5 inches (930 mm)
Weight	9 pounds 3 ounces (4.2 kg)
Range	approximately 1000 yards
Calibre	.577
Magazine	none: single-shot breech-loader
Rate of fire	approximately ten rounds per minute

In August 1864 a Board of Ordnance committee began to investigate the production of *breech-loading* rifles, since these would be faster to load and use in action. Trials of mechanisms by different designers at Woolwich Arsenal led to the adoption in September 1866 of the system devised by Jacob Snider, a New York gun-maker. It was the first breech-loader to be accepted into general use with the British Army. At first, existing 1853 Pattern .577 Enfield rifles were simply converted to accept the new Snider breech-loading system (and designated the Pattern I Snider-Enfield rifle) though within a few years Snider breech-loaders were being constructed in their own right. As usual there were a number of later variations and adaptations to the basic type, with slightly differing versions produced for the Navy, the Volunteers, the Yeomanry, colonial forces, the Cadets and police, as well as carbine versions for cavalry and artillery use.

A key development that enabled the successful introduction of the breech-loading mechanism was that of the metal

Left: *The Snider-Enfield percussion rifle, c.1867, was the first breech-loader adopted by the British Army, at a time when continental powers such as France and Prussia were making great strides in the development of similar weapons.*

Below: *A section through the Snider breech. In this system the hammer strikes a bar or pin, which in turn hits a detonator cap within the cartridge base, detonating the charge and firing the bullet. A separate percussion cap was not required.*

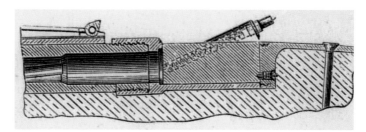

The Snider-Enfield with breech open.

cartridge – a sealed container with detonator cap, gunpowder charge and bullet, which was pushed into the breech with the thumb. When the trigger was pulled, the hammer descended on to a central striker-rod, which was driven into the cartridge and detonated the charge. The brass cartridge case expanded into the breech, providing a gas seal behind the bullet. Early Sniders initially used metal cartridges designed by J. E. Schneider but the Army quickly adopted rolled-brass cartridges designed by Colonel Edward Boxer, which continued in use with the Martini-Henry rifle into the 1880s.

The breech of the Snider-Enfield in closed, 'fired', position. Note the maker's marks: London Small Arms Company, dated 1868.

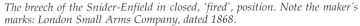

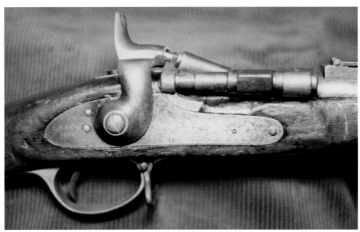

The Martini-Henry rifle, 1874.

The Martini-Henry rifle, 1874–c.1895

Overall length	49 inches (1245 mm)
Barrel length	33.2 inches (844.5 mm)
Weight	8 pounds 12 ounces (3.97 kg)
Range	sighted up to 1300 yards
Calibre	.45
Magazine	none: single-shot breech-loader
Rate of fire	approximately twelve rounds per minute

The introduction of the Snider breech-loader was not seen as a long-term solution, given the advance in infantry weapons in mainland Europe. A committee set up in 1866 to examine the development of the breech-loader tested various weapons between 1868 and 1870 and eventually recommended the adoption of the Martini-Henry rifle in September 1871. The Mark I, which went into mass production in 1874, was a revolutionary weapon in its day. The 'falling-block' breech action with central firing-pin was designed by a former lace-maker from Austria, Friedrich Martini, and the seven-groove rifling by Alexander Henry, a gun-maker from Edinburgh. It used the centre-fire rolled-brass Boxer cartridge.

Although the Martini-Henry was very powerful and accurate over a much longer range than its predecessors, it had a number of well-publicised failings – it had a severe 'kick', it tended to overheat

A soldier of The Scottish Rifles (Cameronians) armed with a Martini-Henry rifle.

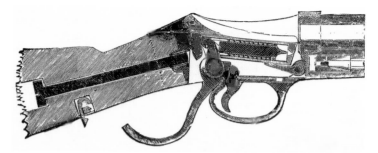

Above: *A cross-section through the breech of the Martini-Henry, showing the 'falling-block' mechanism, operated by depressing the under-lever. This ejected the spent cartridge and revealed the breech chamber, ready to receive a new cartridge.*

Right: *Typical 'bottle-neck' Boxer brass cartridges as used in the Martini-Henry. Those shown, in relic condition, were recovered from the battlefield of Isandhlwana in Zululand. This disastrous battle, fought on 22nd January 1879, proved that a European army equipped with the most up-to-date weapons was not always a match for less well-armed opponents.*

Below: *Soldiers of the Army Service Corps, c.1888, armed with Martini-Henry carbines. The short carbine, usually with a long 'sword-bayonet', was particularly practical for soldiers on horseback or those driving wagons or carts.*

Left: *The Martini-Henry with breech open, ready to be loaded. The version shown here is the Mark II of 1876. It bears the Enfield factory markings.*

Below: *The Martini-Henry with breech closed, ready to be fired.*

quickly and to foul easily. Its most dangerous failing, however, was the tendency for the thin brass cartridge to jam in the breech when being extracted – not very pleasant for a soldier 'in action'. This was reported in the Zulu War and in the Sudan. Nevertheless, the rifle went through a number of alterations and remained, in various marks, the standard infantry weapon of the British soldier through well-known imperial campaigns such as those in Afghanistan in 1878–80, Zululand in 1879, Egypt and the Sudan in 1882–5, the North West Frontier of India and Burma in 1885–7. It was also used by the Indian and Egyptian armies and remained in service with them and with other colonial forces until beyond the end of the century – much longer than its lifespan with the British Army.

Indian soldiers armed with the Martini-Henry rifle. As with other versions of British rifles, the Martini-Henry remained in service in India and the colonies long after it had been replaced in the British Army by more modern weapons such as the Lee-Metford and Lee-Enfield rifles.

Bolt-action magazine rifles

The Lee-Metford rifle, 1888–98

Overall length	49.5 inches (1257 mm)
Barrel length	30.2 inches (767 mm)
Empty weight	9 pounds 5 ounces (4.22 kg)
Range	up to 2900 yards
Calibre	.303
Magazine	initially holding eight .303 rounds; enlarged to hold ten in 1892
Rate of fire	approximately twenty-five rounds per minute using the magazine

Whatever the merits of the Martini-Henry, its deficiencies were serious. As a result, during the 1880s the Board of Ordnance experimented with a range of new rifle systems, which included combinations of the Martini 'falling-block' breech mechanism with rifling types designed at the Enfield factory and by the inventor and engineer William Metford. Various breech and rifling combinations, known as 'Enfield-Martinis' and 'Martini-Metfords', were produced for trial use between 1886 and 1895 and some were actually issued to colonial forces.

However, the British Arms Committee report of 1887 did not favour the continuance (in whatever combination) of the Martini mechanism, but recommended the adoption of a completely new *bolt-action* system. The result was the Lee-Metford rifle. This coupled a bolt-action and box-magazine system devised by James Paris Lee (1831–1904), a Scottish-born American arms inventor, with the rifling design of William Ellis Metford (1824–99), an English civil engineer.

The new rifle was of a smaller calibre than any before and used a rimmed .303 brass cartridge based on designs by a Swiss officer, Major Rubin, adapted by Metford and tested at Woolwich in 1887. Metford's rifling was designed to accommodate the new cartridge and bullet and was less subject to fouling by the gunpowder then available.

Lee-Metford British Magazine Rifle.

A contemporary woodcut showing the breech section of the Lee-Metford rifle. This was the first bolt-action magazine rifle to be used by the British Army and the first to use the .303 brass cartridge of a type which was to remain in use into the mid 1950s.

A soldier of The Rifle Brigade armed with a Lee-Metford rifle, c.1890.

This .303 ammunition with various modifications (mainly to the coating of the lead bullet) was to remain in use with the British Army for over seventy years and was not superseded until the adoption of the self-loading rifle (see page 34) with its 7.62 mm NATO-standard ammunition in 1957.

Lee-Metford rifles were largely manufactured by the Royal Small Arms Factories in Enfield and Birmingham and went through a number of patterns or versions between the first model, the Mark I, which went into production in December 1888, and the Mark II* of April 1895 – a weapon that was used extensively in the Sudan campaign of 1896–8. Carbine versions produced from 1894 were based on the Mark II but with a six-round magazine.

Left: *In this photograph of c.1890 a soldier of the Grenadier Guards is armed with a Lee-Metford rifle, carrying the short 'leaf' bayonet designed for it. These were very much more like the 'fighting knife' style of bayonet carried on more recent weapons such as the self-loading rifle and the SA80.*

Right: *A typical .303 round (this one dating from 1943) of the type first introduced in 1887–8 and which continued in service well into the 1950s.*

The 'long' Lee-Enfield rifle, 1895–1903

Overall length	49.4 inches (1255 mm)
Barrel length	30.2 inches (767 mm)
Empty weight	9 pounds 4 ounces (4.35 kg)
Range	up to 2800 yards
Calibre	.303
Magazine	ten rounds
Rate of fire	approximately twenty-five rounds per minute using the magazine

The replacement of gunpowder by a powerful new propellant, cordite, invented in 1889, forced significant changes in the rifling of barrels and in the composition of cartridges. Unlike its predecessors, cordite created virtually no residue to foul the barrel and clog the rifling but was much more powerful and therefore wearing on the barrel, so that a new system of rifling (designed at Enfield) had to be adopted. The new barrels

were combined with the Lee bolt and magazine action to produce the Lee-Enfield rifle. The first, Mark I, was introduced in November 1895 and was similar to the older Lee-Metford Mark II* but with a new five-groove rifling. A second type, the Lee-Enfield Mark I*, introduced in May 1899, was similar except that the cleaning rod was removed; the use of

Above: The breech section of the 'long' Lee-Enfield, showing the magazine and with the bolt in closed position.

Right: The breech section of the 'long' Lee-Enfield, showing the magazine and with the bolt drawn back in open position.

Right: The breech section of the 'long' Lee-Enfield, showing the magazine and with the bolt in closed position. This example has a metal dust cover protecting the bolt action. The cover plate is attached to the bolt and withdraws with it when the bolt is pulled back.

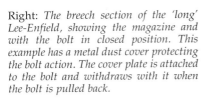

The 'long' Lee-Enfield in use: Private Saville of the 2nd Lancashire Fusiliers in South Africa in 1902, at the end of the Boer War.

cordite rendered the old ramrod system of cleaning the barrel unnecessary and a less harsh cord and cloth pull-through could be employed. Since cordite burned at a much higher temperature than powder, a simple lead bullet was no longer suitable and the .303 bullets for these rifles were hardened with a 'jacket' (coating) of cupro-nickel. A carbine version was produced in 1896.

This rifle was the standard British long-arm of the Boer War (1899–1902) though it should be borne in mind that earlier versions of other rifles – such as Lee-Metfords and even Martini-Henrys – remained in use, especially with colonial forces in South Africa and elsewhere, or with the Volunteers and Militia, all of whom tended to be less well armed

Right: *The fore-sight on a 'long' Lee-Enfield. Most British rifles carried a simple front sight like this – indeed, firearms had carried a 'bead' front sight since at least the mid fifteenth century. Note the bayonet attachment below the barrel.*

Below left and right: *Rear sights: laid flat and raised. Sights like these were used from the Enfield rifle through to the end of the SMLE series. As weapons became more accurate over a long range, specialised sights were needed. These adjustable 'gallows' sights, usually about 12 inches (32 cm) from the eye, enabled the soldier to aim over a greater distance using the moveable 'leaf' slider and the fore-sight.*

The 'long' Lee-Enfield still in use: the demand for rifles at the outbreak of the First World War was so great that many recruits were issued with old 'long' Lee-Enfields for training purposes, even though they had been superseded by the SMLE.

than their contemporaries in the Regular forces.

The rifles were manufactured in Britain by the Royal Small Arms Factories at Enfield and Sparkbrook in Birmingham, by the Birmingham and London Small Arms Companies, and at the Lithgow Rifle Factory in Australia and the Ishapore Arsenal in India.

The 'short' Lee-Enfield rifle, 1902–57

Length overall	initially 44.5 inches (1130 mm) but many later variations
Barrel length	initially 25.19 inches (643 mm) but many later variations
Empty weight	initially 8 pounds 10 ounces (3.85 kg) but many later variations
Range	up to 2800 yards
Calibre	.303
Magazine	ten rounds
Rate of fire	fifteen rounds per minute normal, twenty-five 'rapid fire'

One of the most celebrated weapons of all time was the 'short' magazine Lee-Enfield, or 'SMLE' as it is

A young-looking soldier of The King's Shropshire Light Infantry in 1914. He is armed with the SMLE, which carries the standard 1913 Enfield sword-bayonet.

The butt-plate of a Lee-Enfield rifle. Metal plates were used to strengthen the butt from at least the time of the Brown Bess through to the first types of self-loading rifle. From c.1899 they also housed a compartment or 'trap' – shown here – which held cleaning materials such as pieces of cloth and a cord 'pull-through', for the barrel.

familiarly known, which remained in use in one form or another for over fifty years. It rendered outstanding service with British and Imperial forces in two world wars, in the Korean War and in post-war imperial conflicts such as in Malaya and Kenya. Indeed, later versions of this familiar rifle are still in service with the armed forces of a number of countries.

At the end of the Boer War, in which the role of the lightly armed, mobile soldier had been brought to the fore, it was intended to create a lighter weapon that combined the standard infantryman's arm with the cavalry carbine and was usable by infantry and mounted soldiers alike. The result – the SMLE Mark I – was universally decried as being neither one thing nor the other: too short for long-range accuracy, too long to use from horseback, and too complicated to manufacture. Nevertheless, to a chorus of universal criticism, the Mark I, with its familiar 'all round' wooden furniture and snub nose, went into production in July 1903.

The rifle went through many variants during its long life, from the initial Mark I of July 1903, through Mark I*, which incorporated a receptacle or 'trap' built into the butt to hold

An officer and men of the Machine Gun Corps with SMLEs on the Somme in 1916. Two marks are shown here – the Mark III to the right and the Mark I in the centre. (IWM Q1555)

Two sergeants of The Royal Fusiliers in 1915, in full Field Service Marching Order, with their SMLE rifles.

cleaning materials, via the Mark II Conversion (November 1903), which was an alteration of Mark I and earlier Lee-Metfords, with new sights and shorter, lighter barrels. The idea of *charger-loading* – the ability to load a pre-set 'clip' of five rounds into the ten-round magazine to save time – was first introduced with this version (for an illustration of an example see page 37). Other marks and conversions altered the sights and weight of the rifle, while three conversions, all of October 1909, were refinements of Mark I** types and were introduced only for use by the Royal Navy. Mark I*** (22nd August 1914) was introduced just after the outbreak of war and offered improvements to the sights and the adoption of a new, pointed, Mark 7 bullet, replacing the older round-nose Mark 6 types.

The First World War produced such a demand for weapons that rifles of all kinds, British and foreign, old and new, were put into service. However, the 1907 Mark III SMLE and its wartime variants (such as the Mark III* of January 1916, with the magazine shape and other components simplified to aid mass production) was *the* standard British infantry rifle of the 'Great War'. It was very well thought of by those who used it – reliable, accurate and fast to load and fire. Approximately three million were produced by a range of manufacturers in the United Kingdom and overseas and it remained in use well into the Second World War.

The SMLE Mark III.

The Ross rifle, 1915. The demand for rifles was so great during the First World War that obsolete weapons were re-issued and foreign-made (for example, United States and Canadian) ones adopted. The Ross was manufactured in Canada by the Ross Rifle Company, having been designed by a Scottish baronet, Sir Charles Ross, following Austrian patterns. It was used by Canadian and British troops but was discontinued in 1917. Many were re-issued to the Home Guard in 1940.

Left: *The Somme, 1916: soldiers in a dug-out with their SMLEs to hand. Note the waterproof covers protecting the breech mechanism. They carry the long Enfield sword-bayonet, the standard British bayonet of the 1914–18 war. (IWM Q4012)*

Right: *A marksman of The King's Shropshire Light Infantry, the winner of the Luckock Cup for rifle shooting in India, in 1935. He is armed with the Number 1 rifle.*

Soldiers in Italy in 1943. Most of the men carry Thompson sub-machine guns, but the central figure carries the old SMLE Mark III with the Enfield sword-bayonet. Shorter 'spike bayonets' were more frequently used in the Second World War.

FIRING POSITION—KNEELING

LEFT ELBOW RESTING
BEHIND OR IN FRONT
OF THE KNEE-CAP

An illustration from a 1941 Home Guard training manual showing the firing position when kneeling. The old Pattern 1914 or Number 3 rifle is shown; it remained in use with the Home Guard after it had been withdrawn as obsolete from the Regular Army.

By the end of the 1914–18 war the many adaptations of the SMLE had produced a bewildering range of marks and variants, so it was decided to simplify its designation. In 1926 the existing SMLE then in use as the standard British rifle – essentially the Mark III – was renamed the **Number 1 rifle** and remained in use with the Regular Army until 1941 and with auxiliary forces for longer than that. The **Number 2 rifle** was simply a modified version of the Number 1, firing .22 bullets, for use by Cadets.

What was designated in 1941 as the **Number 3 rifle** began life in 1911–13 as an experimental 'Pattern 1913' SMLE with smaller .286 calibre but was not put into production. However, during the First World War this rifle (then designated the **Pattern 1914**) was adapted to take standard .303 rounds. Some, fitted with a telescopic sight, were issued to meet the need for a sniper rifle. During the latter stages of the war many were produced for the British government in the United States (for example, by the Remington and Winchester companies) and they were also adopted by the Americans, but using their smaller .300 round. Number 3 rifles were issued to the Home Guard in the Second World War but were declared obsolete in 1947.

The Number 4 rifle, as used in the Second World War. More of the barrel protrudes from the furniture so that it lacks the familiar 'snub-nose' look of earlier SMLEs. The version shown here, with the bolt drawn back and rear-sight raised, is of American manufacture, produced by the Stevens Company of Massachusetts and made available to Britain under the 'lease-lend' scheme.

British soldiers emplaning for Bahrain in 1956 armed with the Number 5 rifle, with its distinctive flared flash-eliminator.

The **Number 4 rifle**, developed in the early 1930s and generally introduced in November 1939, was the standard infantryman's weapon of the Second World War. It was very similar to the old SMLE Mark III but with simplified construction (which aided wartime mass production) and alterations to the sights; more of the barrel was exposed beyond the furniture and there were attachment lugs for the new 'spike' bayonet. About four million were produced.

The **Number 5 rifle**, developed in 1943 and introduced into service in September 1944, was a shorter, lighter version of the Number 4, originally designed for use in jungle conditions in the Far East and sometimes called the 'jungle carbine'. Its overall length was only 3 feet $3^1/2$ inches (1000 mm) and it had a distinctive flared flash-eliminator on the muzzle.

Later experimental variants – the **Number 6**, **Number 7** and **Number 8** rifles – were never put into production before self-loading rifles came into use.

The Number 5 rifle, with its characteristic flared muzzle. This version – smaller and lighter than previous marks of SMLE – was produced for use in the jungles of Burma and Malaya. Also shown is the short knife-bayonet associated with this weapon.

Automatic rifles

The Self-Loading Rifle (L1A1), 1957–85

Overall length	45 inches (1053 mm)
Barrel length	21 inches (533 mm)
Empty weight	9.5 pounds (4.3 kg)
Range	sighted to 600 yards
Calibre	7.62 mm
Magazine	twenty rounds
Rate of fire	up to 650 rounds per minute

Manual, bolt-action Enfield rifles had seen service for over fifty years by the end of the Second World War. But new concepts of warfare called for lighter, faster-shooting weapons than these old standards. Attempts had been made as early as the 1880s to develop self-loading rifles, in which the action was cocked, spent cartridges were automatically ejected and a new live round was lifted into the breech *without* the manual operation of a bolt. However, it was not until the 1930s that an effective self-loading rifle appeared in the form of the American Garand. As a result of the impetus given by the Second World War, German and Russian types were also developed, but the British did not enter the scene until after the war.

The British version produced at Enfield in the late 1940s was the EMII or '**Rifle, Automatic Number 9, Mark 1**', to give it its full designation. Although it was a well-regarded weapon, of 'bullpup' (light, stocky) style, gas-operated and of a small, .280, calibre, it never went into service with the British Army. At a time when Britain was playing a leading role in setting up the

A comparison of rounds: from left to right, the .303 (used from 1895 to 1956), the 7.62 (used in the SLR from 1956 to 1985) and the 5.62 round of the SA80. Notice that the bullet becomes progressively smaller.

The experimental EMII: Britain's first attempt at a self-loading rifle, which came to nothing with the adoption of the Belgian FAL. An early example of the short, stocky 'bullpup' design that was adopted with the SA80 (see page 38) in 1985.

NATO alliance its light calibre did not find favour and the British government instead chose to adapt a new Belgian design. Originally produced by the main Belgian arms factory, the Fabrique Nationale d'Armes de Guerre (FN), this revolutionary weapon, light, sturdy, accurate and simple to

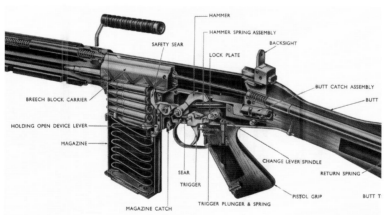

A cut-away section of the Self-Loading Rifle (L1A1), based on the Belgian FAL, showing breech mechanisms.

The SLR: two views of the weapon.

Loading the magazine of the SLR: from a contemporary manual.

maintain, was the FAL – the *fusil automatique léger* (light automatic rifle), designed in 1950. It was sold to more than ninety nations and produced under licence in many countries, including most of the NATO allies at some time or other. It is still in use with many armies around the world.

The FAL, or SLR as it was universally known, used a gas-actuated mechanism to eject the spent cartridge, load the next round into the breech and cock the mechanism. It could be used in automatic-fire or selective-fire mode.

Soldiers armed with the SLR on exercise. The type shown here has the wooden furniture (butt, pistol-grip and stock) of the original rifles.

The later SLR, with all-plastic furniture, which came into use in the 1970s.

A close-up of the pistol-grip and magazine of the SLR.

Those produced for the British Army were designated **L1A1**s and they remained the standard British service rifle until replaced by the L85A1 – the current British infantry rifle – which came into general service in 1987.

The pistol-grip and magazine of the SLR in the version with plastic furniture. In this photograph the weapon's carrying handle is raised.

RESTRICTED	W.O. Code
The information given in this document is not to be communicated, either directly or indirectly, to the Press or to any person not authorized to receive it.	No. 12258

User Handbook

for the

RIFLE, 7·62mm., L1A1

**Land Service
1959**

(Prepared by Ministry of Supply)

By Command of the Army Council

E. W. Playfair

THE WAR OFFICE

A clip of five rounds of 7.52 ammunition for the SLR.

An official handbook for the SLR – typical of the handbooks available for all versions of rifles used by the British Army since the late nineteenth century.

On exercise in Malaya in 1967: this British soldier is armed with an American M16 rifle. The British Army uses non-standard weapons if they are a better match for the weapons soldiers may have to defend themselves against. British soldiers on duty in Northern Ireland have also used M16 rifles.

The SA80 (L85A1), 1985 to date

Overall length	30.9 inches (785 mm)
Barrel length	20.4 inches (518 mm)
Empty weight	10.98 pounds (4.98 kg)
Range	sighted to 500 yards
Calibre	5.56 mm
Magazine	30 rounds
Rate of fire	up to 700 rounds per minute

The present British service rifle – or 'individual weapon' to use the current jargon – is the L85A1, commonly called the SA80 ('small arm for the 1980s'). Submitted for NATO trials in 1977, it first entered service in the British Army in 1985. The weapon, designed from the outset with battlefield practicalities in mind, is of light, 'bullpup' design, can be fired in semi-automatic or automatic mode and uses a light, 5.56 mm, NATO-standard round. The rifle is issued to combat units with a special x 4 optical sight (the SUSAT – Sight Unit, Small Arm, Trilux) but can also carry more basic iron sights, which are issued as standard to support units. The body and parts are made of welded steel and the furniture entirely of high-impact plastic,

Above: *A Light Infantryman on exercise in Jordan. His SA80 is fitted with the SUSAT optical sight and the short knife-bayonet, which also serves as a multi-purpose tool.*

with a great deal of attention going into balance and the placing of grips and sights.

The rifle gained a degree of notoriety in its early years in the wake of many well-publicised failings – weakness of construction, complicated mechanisms and ease of jamming (such as in sand). There were calls for the British Army to adopt current American weapons, which were of known reliability, rather than spending millions on altering the new rifle. However, time and money *were* expended on alterations – in particular at

Soldiers on exercise in Belize, carrying the SA80 rifle, in this case with its simple iron sights and with a plastic blank-firing adaptor (BFA), which allows the weapon's gas-operated system to function while firing blank bullets.

The SA80, left side view, showing the pistol-grip and magazine. This weapon has the simple iron sights.

Right: *The SA80 in action, showing the cartridge cases being ejected from the right-hand side of the weapon. It is not possible to fire this rifle from the left shoulder because of this ejection process.*

Below: *Training with the latest type of SA80 (the A2) in Iraq in 2004. The first version of the weapon was heavily criticised for its weak construction and its tendency to jam in sandy or dusty conditions, but the latest version seems to have overcome these problems.*

A soldier of The Light Infantry on patrol in Basra in 2004 armed with the current SA80, with SUSAT optical sight.

the new factory in Nottingham – and the latest version of the weapon (the L85A2) has performed well in British operations (for instance in Iraq). It is well regarded for its lightness, ease of use and accuracy.

A light machine-gun version of the SA80, known as the Light Support Weapon (LSW), has a heavier barrel and bipod stand. In design and operation it is similar to the SA80, which means that troops trained in the use of the rifle can easily adapt to use the machine-gun.

A clip of ten 5.62 NATO-standard rounds as used with the SA80.

Carbines

Carbines are essentially lighter, cut-down versions of the current infantry long-arm, for use by mounted soldiers. They were carried by some cavalry units (such as the Dragoons), some Yeomanry regiments and by specialist troops, such as drivers of the Royal Artillery, the Royal Engineers and Army transport services. They were intended to be more convenient to use from horseback or horse-drawn transport.

Carbines were first used by British cavalry in the mid eighteenth century and were simply shorter versions of the Brown Bess and with a smaller bore. Flintlock carbines varied considerably, however, over the next hundred years in barrel lengths, size of bore, weight and range. Often carbines fired a ball of the same weight and calibre as a contemporary pistol.

A shooting team of the Surma Valley Light Horse in India, armed with Martini-Henry carbines, which remained in use to the end of the nineteenth century. Some were still in service with the British Army and Colonial forces in South Africa during the Boer War.

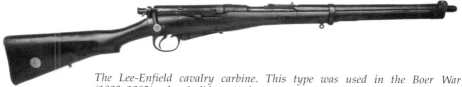

The Lee-Enfield cavalry carbine. This type was used in the Boer War (1899–1902), when it did not perform to general satisfaction.

Perhaps the best-known early carbine was the Paget, invented in 1800 by Lord Paget, a British cavalry commander of the Napoleonic Wars. It had a very short barrel (16 inches), which made it light to carry and use, and an attached ramrod that could not fall off. It was very successful and remained in use until the end of the flintlock era, c.1840.

Carbine versions of all the standard infantry rifles for use by artillery, engineers, cavalry, police and colonial mounted troops were produced throughout the nineteenth century, but the Boer War (1899–1902) was the last occasion on which British

A soldier of the Yeomanry, c.1908. As carbines were no longer used after the Boer War, mounted troops carried standard infantry rifles, in this case the 'long' Lee-Enfield. This photograph clearly shows the 'bucket' which held the rifle-butt.

A Shropshire Yeoman of 1914 'ready for war'. Like all Yeomen and other mounted troops since the end of the Boer War, he carries the standard infantry rifle, in this case the SMLE, rather than a carbine.

mounted troops used them. Although Lee-Enfield carbines had been produced since 1896, Martini-Henry types were still in use with many cavalry regiments. Neither proved any match for modern Boer long-arms (especially the standard Boer rifle, the German 1898-pattern Mauser) and both compared badly in range and accuracy with the standard Lee-Enfields then in use. It was therefore decided in 1902 to abolish the carbine altogether so that, from then on, all branches of the British Army would use the standard long-arm of the day. The new Lee-Enfield SMLE (see page 28) of 1903 was the first rifle designed to meet the requirement for a weapon suitable for use by all arms, and with its adoption the carbine vanished from use in the British Army.

However, it is interesting to note that the production of a smaller version of the current SA80, for use, for example, by tank crews, has been proposed – and would effectively mark the rebirth of the British carbine after a hundred years!

Places to visit and further reading

There are many places in Britain where the researcher or collector can see a good range of British rifles. The Royal Armouries collection of firearms, formerly housed in the Tower of London – a place long associated with the British firearms industry as a store and a manufactory – has largely been moved to its new outstation, the Royal Armouries Museum in Leeds, which displays a very fine and comprehensive collection. The very important reference collection of firearms constituting the Ministry of Defence Pattern Room at the Royal Small Arms Factory at Enfield (and later in the RSAF at Nottingham) has also moved to the Royal Armouries in Leeds. However, specialist researchers who wish to view a weapon displayed in the Royal Armouries in Leeds can, by arrangement, have it brought to the Tower of London, if this is more convenient.

Both the National Army Museum and the Imperial War Museum have comprehensive collections on view or available for reference. Specialist museums – whether large institutions such as the Royal Engineers Museum, or local regimental collections – will often have good selections of the basic types of rifle used by the British Army; consult *A Guide to Military Museums* by T. and S. Wise (Imperial Press,

Left and above: *From the earliest times barrels have been 'proofed' (in other words, proven sound – fired as a test of barrel and breech strength). This was commonly done at the Ordnance proof-house at the Tower of London but later also by private arms factories (for example, in Birmingham). A law of 1855 made proofing compulsory for all firearms sold in Britain. Weapons were stamped with various marks – as shown here – to indicate that they had been tested, re-tested or inspected and had met the necessary standard.*

Knighton) for details of over 150 such museums throughout the United Kingdom.

The Imperial War Museum, Lambeth Road, London SE1 6HZ. Telephone: 020 7416 5320. Website: www.iwm.org.uk

The National Army Museum, Royal Hospital Road, Chelsea, London SW3 4HT. Telephone: 020 7730 0717. Website: www.national-army-museum.ac.uk

The Royal Armouries Museum, Armouries Drive, Leeds LS10 1LT. Telephone: 0113 220 1916. Website: www.armouries.org.uk

The Royal Engineers Museum, Brompton Barracks, Prince Arthur Road, Gillingham, Kent ME4 4UG. Telephone: 01634 822839. Website: www.royalengineers.org.uk

The Tower of London, London EC3N 4AB. Telephone: 0870 756 6060. Website: www.armouries.org.uk or www.hrp.org.uk

The Internet gives access to information on rifle collectors' and users' associations and similar 'forums' (for example, the Lee Enfield Rifle Association; website: www.leeenfieldrifleassociation.org.uk) and on specific weapons and rifles (for example, for the Martini-Henry try the website www.martinihenry.com). However, using a basic search facility on your computer will throw up a wide range of sites covering just about every type of rifle, British and foreign.

A number of collectors' and users' magazines also cater for those interested in rifles; examples are *The International Arms and Militaria Collector* (Arms and Military Press, Labrador, Australia, from 1995) and general militaria magazines such as *The Armourer* (Beaumont Press, Adelphi Mill, Bollington, Cheshire SK10 5JB; telephone: 01625 575700; website: www.armourer.co.uk). There is equally a wide range of reference works now available on rifles. Some are general, covering a whole era or class of weapon, and some are detailed studies of one particular type. The following is only a brief selection of informative and useful titles.

Baker, Ezekiel. *Remarks on Rifle Guns*. London, 1835.
Blackmore, H. L. *British Military Firearms 1650–1850*. Herbert Jenkins, London, 1961.
HMSO. *British Rifles*. 1981.
Hogg, I. V., and Weeks, J. *Military Small Arms of the Twentieth Century*. Arms & Armour Press, London, 1991.

The Whitworth rifle (c.1858–66). The British Army always experimented with a range of weapons. This .451 rifle with an unusual hexagonal bore was designed by the engineer Sir Joseph Whitworth in response to the Army's request for an improvement on the accuracy of the Enfield. Although renowned for its accuracy over long range – it became a favoured weapon with competition target-shooters – it was not accepted into the British Army because its barrel fouled easily; only The Rifle Brigade used the weapon, and only for a short time, before the Snider-Enfield was generally adopted.

Soldiers of The King's Shropshire Light Infantry mount guard at Buckingham Palace in 1948. They carry the Number 4 Lee-Enfield rifle.

L'Amour, L. *The Ferguson Rifle*. Bantam, New York, 1985.

Markham, G. *Guns of the Empire: Firearms of the British Soldier, 1847–1987*. Arms & Armour Press, London, 1987.

Peterson, H. L. (editor). *The Encyclopaedia of Firearms*. Connoisseur, London, 1964.

Petrillo, A. M. *Cartridge Carbines of the British Army*. Excalibur Publications, London, 1998.

Reynolds, E. G. B. *The Lee Enfield Rifle*. Profile Publications, Windsor, undated.

Rogers, Colonel H. C. B. *Weapons of the British Soldier*. Seeley, London, 1960.

Skennerton, I. D. *The Lee Enfield Story*. Skennerton, Australia, 1993.

Skennerton, I. D., and Temple, B. *A Treatise on the British Military Martini* (three volumes). B. A. Temple, Australia, 1983.

Skennerton, I. D., and Temple, B. *The Small Arms Identification* series – comprises a range of detailed pamphlets on various British weapons. Skennerton, Australia, 1990s.

The War Office. *User Handbooks* – for all major rifle types since the 1870s.

Index